So You Think

w

re?

The Definitive Shakespeare Quiz Book

John & Claire Saunders

ABOUT THE AUTHORS

Claire and John Saunders met in Oxford whilst helping to run a Literature Summer School. They moved to Chichester, in West Sussex (where Laurence Olivier had recently established the now world-famous Festival Theatre), where they have lived ever since.

Following an Oxford degree in English Language and Literature, Claire taught at University College, Dublin. After marrying, she combined bringing up children with taking a further degree in Renaissance Literature, tutoring for the Open University and school teaching. She has contributed to various educational and academic publications, mainly on Shakespeare.

John Saunders has post-graduate degrees from Oxford, Cambridge and London. While lecturing at University College, Chichester, he specialised in the teaching of Shakespeare, Film Studies and Creative Writing. He has edited several Shakespeare texts and has written and reviewed for a number of academic publications. He has been a regular contributor to conferences on literature and the arts and has taught at the Stratford-upon-Avon Summer School on the Teaching of Shakespeare.

In an earlier collaboration, Claire and John edited John Webster's *The Duchess of Malfi*.

So You Think You Know
Shakespeare?

The Definitive Shakespeare Quiz Book

John & Claire Saunders

Cold Spring Press

Cold Spring Press

P.O. Box 284, Cold Spring Harbor, NY 11724
E-mail: Jopenroad@aol.com

ISBN 1-59360-078-X
Library of Congress Control No. 2006901257

Contents

Introduction

*'To the great variety of readers,
from the most able to those that can but spell'*

That's how Shakespeare's first editors presented him to the world in 1623. And now we're presenting him again – in a very different format but still aiming at a wide range of readers. This book is for Shakespeare enthusiasts, both experts and beginners. All you will need is intelligence, curiosity and a sense of fun.

Here are 20 different quizzes. They cover Shakespeare's use of language as well as characters, events and recurrent motifs. Once you've tackled the lot, you'll have been introduced to every play that Shakespeare wrote, as well as several of his poems, and you'll know why Shakespeare is considered supreme as both poet and dramatist.

The first ten quizzes are interactive, offering you a chance to construct the richly varied quotations on which they're based. Some are famous, some are great. They range from courting to cursing; they include the tender, the witty, the sublime; they cover everything from eating to dying. Then come seven topic-centred quizzes. These deal with such things as Dreams, Villains and Resurrections and show how, throughout his career, Shakespeare developed his ideas and preoccupations. The final three quizzes focus on particular plays – *A Midsummer Night's Dream*, *Hamlet* and *The Tempest* – and they'll really test your knowledge.

You can tackle these quizzes in any order you like. Some of you will be competitive (the highest score in our trials so far has been 289/300 – from a retired professor of English). The first ten quizzes (up to Dying Words) score 20 points each; the remaining ten quizzes score 10 points each. Doing the quizzes in a group or with a partner can be particularly rewarding. And it really is good to read the quotations aloud – Shakespeare is meant to be heard, and sound is often an important guide to meaning.

The second half of the book gives you the answers. Some are a little fuller than strictly necessary and might almost be called educational. But the overall idea is to offer a glimpse of Shakespeare as he should be experienced – inspiring, shocking, beautiful, funny – never pompous.

Good luck!

THE QUIZZES

The Top Ten

(a) **Complete each of the following famous quotations from the three choices on offer:**

1. To be or not to be, that is the ------.

   question   *answer*   *problem*

2.   All the world's a stage
   And all the men and women merely ------.

   actors   *props*   *players*

3. Cowards die many times before their deaths,
   The ------ never taste of death but once.

   heroic   *valiant*   *foolish*

4. The course of true love never did run------.

   quickly   *smoothly*   *smooth*

5. What's in a name? That which we call a ———
   By any other name would smell as sweet.

   violet   *rose*   *lily*

6. The quality of mercy is not strain'd,
   It droppeth as the gentle ------ from heaven.

   manna   *rain*   *peace*

7. A horse, a horse! My ------ for a horse!

   freedom   *wealth*   *kingdom*

8. Shall I compare thee to a ------ day?

   winter's   *summer's*   *spring*

9. Is this a ------ which I see before me,
   The handle toward my hand?

   dagger   *sword*   *knife*

10. O, beware, my lord, of jealousy!
It is the green-ey'd ------ which doth mock
The meat it feeds on.

lobster   *mobster*   *monster*

(b) How many of the speakers of the above quotations can you identify?
Answers from:

Jaques (in *As You Like It*)

Lysander (in *A Midsummer Night's Dream*)

Juliet (in *Romeo and Juliet*)

Julius Caesar (in *Julius Caesar*)

Macbeth (in *Macbeth*)

Iago (in *Othello*)

Hamlet (in *Hamlet*)

Portia (in *The Merchant of Venice*)

Richard III (in *Richard III*)

Shakespeare (in 'Sonnet 18')

ANSWERS BEGIN ON PAGE 65

Opening Words

(a) Complete each of the following openings:

1. Two households, both alike in ------,
   In fair Verona, where we lay our scene.

   wealth   *reputation*   *dignity*

2. Now is the winter of our discontent
   Made glorious summer by this ------ of York.

   moon   *sun*   *son*

3. If music be the food of love, play on,
   Give me excess of it; that surfeiting,
   The appetite may ------, and so die.

   sicken   *climax*   *fade*

4. O for a muse of fire, that would ascend
   The brightest heaven of ------ !

   intervention   *intention*   *invention*

5. When my love swears that she is made of truth,
   I do believe her, though I know she ------.

   exaggerates   *pretends*   *lies*

6. When shall we three meet again?
   In thunder, lightning or in ------?

   vain   *pain*   *rain*

7. In sooth, I know not why I am so ------.

   merry   *sad*   *depressed*

8. So shaken as we are, so ------ with care.

   weary   *over-burdened*   *wan*

9. Let fame, that all hunt after in their lives,
   Live regist'red upon our brazen ------.

   tombs   *wombs*   *combs*

10. Hung be the ------ with black, yield day to night!

stage   *skies*   *heavens*

(b) Can you identify the works from which these openings have been taken? Answers from:

> *Henry IV, Part 1*
>
> *Henry V*
>
> *Henry VI, Part 1*
>
> *Love's Labour's Lost*
>
> *Macbeth*
>
> *The Merchant of Venice*
>
> *Richard III*
>
> *Romeo and Juliet*
>
> *Twelfth Night*
>
> 'Sonnet 138'

ANSWERS BEGIN ON PAGE 67

Courting Couples

(a) Passages 1 to 10 each play their part in a 'courtship' or 'love match'. Passages (a) to (j) are responses – but not in the right order. Can you match the couples?

1. I wonder that you will still be talking [......] nobody marks you. *e*

2. For women are as roses, whose fair flow'r
   Being once display'd, doth fall that very hour *h*

3. An angel is like you, Kate, and you are like an angel. *a*

4. Come, come, you wasp, i' faith you are too angry. *i*

5. If I profane with my unworthiest hand ..... *f*

6. If it be love indeed, tell me how much. *b*

7. What did you swear you would bestow on me? *c*

8. O kiss me through the hole of this vile wall! *j*

9. My prime request, which I do last pronounce,   *g*
   Is (O you wonder!) if you be maid, or no?

10. 'I am,' quoth he, 'expected by my friends,   *d*
    And now 'tis dark, and going I shall fall'.

(a) Pardonnez moi, I cannot tell vat is 'like me'.

(b) There's beggary in the love that can be reckon'd.

(c) I prithee do not hold me to mine oath.

(d) 'In night', quoth she, 'Desire sees best of all.'

(e) What, my dear Lady Disdain! Are you yet living?

(f) Good pilgrim, you do wrong your hand too much …

(g) No wonder, sir, but certainly a maid.

(h) And so they are; alas, that they are so!
     To die, even when they to perfection grow!

(i) If I be waspish, best beware my sting.

(j) I kiss the wall's hole, not your lips at all.

(b) Can you identify the couples? Chose from:

Adonis and Venus (in *Venus and Adonis*) 10

Beatrice and Benedick (in *Much Ado About Nothing*) 1

Cleopatra and Antony (in *Antony and Cleopatra*) 6

Diomed and Cressida (in *Troilus and Cressida*) 7

Ferdinand and Miranda (in *The Tempest*) 9

Henry and Princess Katherine (in *Henry V*) 3

Orsino and Viola (in *Twelfth Night*) 2

Petruchio and Katherina (in *The Taming of the Shrew*) 4

Pyramus and Thisbe (in *A Midsummer Night's Dream*) 8

Romeo and Juliet (in *Romeo and Juliet*) 5

ANSWERS BEGIN ON PAGE 70

Sex Survey

(a) Provide the missing word from the alternatives on offer:

1. If fires be hot, knives sharp, or waters deep,
   Untied I still my virgin ------ will keep.

   vows   *bloom*   *(knot)*

2. Virginity breeds ------ much like a cheese, consumes itself to the very
   paring, and so dies with feeding his own stomach.

   frights   *(mites)*   *blights*   *Parolles*

3. I am one, sir, that comes to tell you your daughter and the Moor are now
   making the beast with two ------.

   heads   *tails*   *(backs)*   *Iago*

4.   Nay, but to live
In the rank sweat of an enseamed bed,
Stew'd in corruption, ------ and making love
Over the nasty sty.

humping   *honeying*   *wallowing*

5. If thou dost break her virgin knot [....] barren hate
Sour-ey'd disdain, and ------ shall bestrew
The union of your bed with weeds so loathly
That you shall hate it both.

concord   (*discord*)   *conflict*

6. Me of my lawful pleasure she restrain'd,
And pray'd me oft forbearance; did it with
A pudency so rosy the sweet view on't
Might well have warm'd old ------

Saturn   *Satan*   *Santa*

7. But to the girdle do the god's inherit,
Beneath is all the ------.

Lear

(*fiends'*)   *friends'*   *witches'*

8. Give them ------, leaving with thee their lust.
   Make use of thy salt hours. Season the slaves
   For tubs and baths; bring down rose-cheek'd youth
   To the tub-fast and the diet.

      pleasure   *pain*   *diseases*

9. Th' expense of spirit in a waste of shame
   Is lust in action, and till action, lust
   Is perjured, murd'rous, bloody, full of blame,
   Savage, extreme, rude, cruel, not to ------.

      rust   *trust*   *thrust*

10. As those that feed grow full, as blossoming time
    That from the seedness the bare fallow brings
    To teeming foison, even so her plenteous womb
    Expresseth his full tilth and ------.

Lucio!

      husbandry   *industry*   *fertility*

(b) **Can you identify the 'speakers' of the above passages? Answers from:**

 Lucio (in *Measure for Measure*)

   Hamlet (in *Hamlet*)

Iago (in *Othello*)

Lear (in *King Lear*)

Marina (in *Pericles*)

Parolles (in *All's Well that Ends Well*)

Posthumus (in *Cymbeline*)

Prospero (in *The Tempest*)

Shakespeare (in 'Sonnet' 129)

Timon (in *Timon of Athens*)

ANSWERS BEGIN
ON PAGE 72

Creatures Great and Small

(a) Can you place the following 'creatures' in the speeches where they belong?

> spider
> beetle
> caterpillars
> butterfly
> worm
> monkeys
> beagle
> spaniel
> boar
> whale

12th Nt. 1. She's a ~~beagle~~ ------ true-bred, and one that adores me.

Merchant 2. It was my turquoise, I had it of Leah when I was a bachelor. I would not have given it for a wilderness of ------. *monkeys*

3. This foul, grim and urchin-snouted ------
   Whose downward eye still looketh for a grave.

Coriolanus 4. Civil dissension is a viperous ------ _worm_
That gnaws the bowels of the commonwealth.

5. I saw him run after a gilded ------ _butterfly_, and when he caught it, he let it go
again.

Hamlet 6. The poor ------ _beetle_ that we tread upon
In corporal sufferance finds a pang as great
As when a giant dies.

W's Tale 7. _spider_ There may be in the cup
A ------ steep'd , and one may drink; depart
And yet partake no venom.

Midsummer 8. The more you beat me, I will fawn on you.
Use me but as your ------ _spaniel_; spurn me, strike me,
Neglect me, lose me; only give me leave,
Unworthy as I am, to follow you.

9. Her fruit trees all unprun'd, her hedges ruin'd,
Her knots disordered and her wholesome herbs
Swarming with ------. _caterpillars_

10.   the belching ------ _whale_
And humming water must o'erwhelm thy corpse,
Lying with simple shells.

(b) Can you identify the plays from which the above quotations have been taken? Answers from:

Coriolanus

Henry VI, Part 1

Measure for Measure

The Merchant of Venice

A Midsummer Night's Dream

Pericles

Richard II

Twelfth Night

Venus and Adonis

The Winter's Tale

ANSWERS BEGIN ON PAGE 75

Feasting

(a) How many of these items of food can you place in their correct quotations?

~~apricocks~~
venison-pasty
wild-boars
~~capon~~
~~bread~~
~~cakes~~
~~crabs~~
parsley
~~baked-meats~~
marchpane

12ᵗʰ Nt.

1. Dost thou think, because thou art virtuous, there shall be no more
cakes ------ and ale?

AYLI

2.   The Justice   *capon*
In fair round belly with good ------ lined.

3. When roasted ------ hiss in the bowl
Then nightly sings the staring owl.

crabs

4. Feed him with ------ and dewberries,
With purple grapes, green figs and mulberries.

apricocks

Midsummer

5. We have hot ------ to dinner; come, gentlemen, I hope we shall drink down all unkindness.

R+J

6. Good thou, save me a piece of ------; and, as thou lov'st me, let the porter let in Susan Grindstone and Nell.

marchpane

7. I know a wench married in an afternoon as she went to the garden for ------ to stuff a rabbit.

parsley

8. Eight ------ roasted whole at a breakfast and but twelve persons there! Is't true?

wild boars

9. The funeral ------ did coldly furnish forth the marriage table.

baked-meats

Hamlet

10. O but a half-penny'orth of ------ to this intolerable deal of sack!

bread

H IV

(b) Can you identify the plays from which these quotations have been taken? Answers from:

As You Like It

Antony and Cleopatra

Hamlet

Henry IV, Part 1

Love's Labour's Lost

The Merry Wives of Windsor

A Midsummer Night's Dream

Romeo and Juliet

The Taming of the Shrew

Twelfth Night

ANSWERS BEGIN ON PAGE 78

'What's in a Name?'

(a) The names of Shakespeare's characters often reveal much about them. What do we learn about the following characters from their names?

Malvolio — *wishes ill on others*
Fortinbras — *strong leader*
Doll Tearsheet — *whore*
Bottom — *ass*
Cordelia — *hung at end*
Hotspur — *hotheaded*
Ajax
Crab — *dog*
Parolles — *talks a lot*
Abhorson — *executioner*

(b) In which of the following plays will you find the above characters?
Choose from:

All's Well That Ends Well   *Parolles*

Hamlet   *Fortinbras*

Henry IV, Part 1   *Hotspur*

Henry IV, Part 2   Doll Tearsheet

King Lear   Cordelia

The Two Gentlemen of Verona   Crab

Measure for Measure   Abhorson

A Midsummer Night's Dream   Bottom

Troilus and Cressida   Ajax

Twelfth Night   Malvolio

ANSWERS BEGIN ON
PAGE 80

Curses and Insults

(a) From the offered alternatives, complete the following:

1. God hath given you one ------, and you make yourselves another. You
   jig and amble and you lisp, you nickname God's creatures and make
   your wantonness your ignorance.

   Hamlet

   complexion   *face*   *bust*

2.   You are pictures out of doors,
   Bells in your parlours, wild-cats in your kitchens,
   Saints in your injuries, devils being offended,
   Players in your housewifery, housewives in your ------.

   homes   *heads*   *beds*

3. If he were open'd and you find so much blood in his liver as will clog the
   foot of a ------, I'll eat the rest of the anatomy.

   Beatrice

   flea   *leprechaun*   *mouse*

Lucio

4. Some report a sea-maid spawn'd him; some that he was begot between two stock-fishes. But it is certain that when he makes water, his urine is congealed ------ .

custard   frog spawn   ice

5. Have you not a moist eye, a dry hand, a yellow cheek, a white beard, a decreasing leg, an increasing belly? Is not your voice broken, your wind short, your chin ------, your wit single, and every part about you blasted with antiquity.

dimpled   dribbled   double

Q Elizabeth

6. That bottled spider, that foul bunch'd back ------ toad

lord   load   toad

7. You common cry of curs, whose breath I hate
As reek o' the rotten fens, whose loves I prize
As the dead carcasses of unburied men
That do ------ my air.

infect   pollute   corrupt

Lear

8. Into her ------ convey sterility.
   Dry up in her the organs of increase,
   And from her derogate body, never spring
   A babe to honour her!

   heart    *womb*   *body*

9.   Son of sixteen,
   Pluck the lined crutch from thy old limping sire,
   With it beat out his ------.

    *brains*   *wits*   *eyes*

10. Now the rotten diseases of the south, the guts-griping ruptures, catarrhs,
    loads a' gravel in the back, lethargies, cold palsies, raw eyes, dirt-rotten
    livers, whissing ------, bladders full of imposthume, sciaticas, lime kilns
    i' th' palm, incurable bone-ache, and the rivell'd fee-simple of the tetter,
    take and take again such preposterous discoveries.

    wings   *tongues*   *lungs*

(b) How many of the above speakers can you identify? Choose from:

    Chief Justice (in *Henry IV, Part 2*)

    Coriolanus (in *Coriolanus*)

Hamlet (in *Hamlet*)

Iago (in *Othello*)

Lear (in *King Lear*)

Lucio (in *Measure for Measure*)

Queen Elizabeth (in *Richard III*)

Sir Toby Belch (in *Twelfth Night*)

Thersites (in *Troilus and Cressida*)

Timon (in *Timon of Athens*)

ANSWERS BEGIN ON PAGE 82

Similes

(a) **From the ten words below, provide the missing term in each of the similes which follow:**

~~sacrifices~~
~~comet~~
~~babe~~
sleep
~~sun~~
Colossus
flies
drops
rats
~~host~~

1. See, see King [.....] doth himself appear,
   As doth the blushing discontented --Sun--
   From out the fiery portals of the east.

2. By being seldom seen, I could not stir
   But like a ------ I was wondered at.
   Comet

3.   *sacrifices* The poor condemned English,
    Like ------, by their watchful fires
    Sit patiently and inly ruminate.

Chorus

4. And pity, like a naked new-born *babe* ------
    Striding the blast, or heaven's cherubin, hors'd
    Upon the sightless couriers of the air,
    Shall blow the horrid deed in every eye,
    That tears shall drown the wind.

Macb.

5. For time is like a fashionable *host* -------
    That slightly shakes his parting guest by th' hand,
    And with his arms outstretched as he would fly
    Grasps in the comer.

6. He doth bestride the narrow world
    Like a ------, *Colossus* and we petty men
    Walk under his huge legs, and peep about
    To find ourselves dishonourable graves.

7. As *flies* ------ to wanton boys are we to th' gods,
    They kill us for their sport.

8.   On her left breast
    A mole cinque-spotted, like the crimson ------
    I' th' bottom of a cowslip.

9. She looks like ------,
    As she would catch another Antony
    In her strong toil of grace.

10. _rats_ Our natures do pursue,
    Like ------ that ravin down their proper bane,
    A thirsty evil; and when we drink we die.

(b) How many of the works from which the above similes have been taken can you identify? Choose from:

Antony and Cleopatra

Cymbeline

Henry IV, Part 1

Henry V

Julius Caesar

King Lear

Macbeth

Measure for Measure

Richard II

Troilus and Cressida

ANSWERS
BEGIN ON
PAGE 85

Dying Words

(a) Complete each of the following speeches:

1. Mount, mount, my soul, my seat is up on high;
   Whilst my gross ------ sinks downward, here to die.

    body   *flesh*   *ghost*

2. Now am I dead,
   Now am I fled;
   My soul is in the ------.

                clouds   *heavens*

3. I am a scribbled form drawn with a pen
   Upon a parchment, and against this fire
   Do I ------ up.

    burn   *scorch*   *shrink*

4. Pray you undo this button. Thank you, sir.
   Do you see this? Look on her. Look, her ------.
   Look there, look there!

   ears　　　　　*neck*　　　　　*lips*

5. Ask for me tomorrow, and you shall
   find me a ------ man.

   brave　　　　　*grave*　　　　　*saved*

6. Dost thou not see my baby at my breast,
   That ------ the nurse asleep?

   bites　　　　　*sucks*　　　　　*sings*

7. I took by the throat th'uncircumcised ------
   And slew him, thus!

   dog　　　　　*hog*　　　　　*frog*

8. 　　　　　O, I could prophesy,
   But that the icy and cold hand of death
   Lies on my ------.

   heart　　　　　*tongue*　　　　　*breast*

9. I, that never feared any, am vanquished by famine,
   not by ------.

   hunger   *valour*   *virtue*

10. The rest is ------.

   history   *nonsense*   *silence*

(b) **Can you name the speakers? Choose from:**

   Bottom/Pyramus (in *A Midsummer Night's Dream*)

   Cleopatra (in *Antony and Cleopatra*)

   Hamlet (in *Hamlet*)

   Hotspur (in *Henry IV, Part 1*)

   Jack Cade (in *Henry VI, Part 2*)

   King John (in *King John*)

   Lear (in *King Lear*)

   Othello (in *Othello*)

   Richard II (in *Richard II*)

   Mercutio (in *Romeo and Juliet*)

ANSWERS BEGIN
ON PAGE 88

Resurrections

Who:

1. revived in her own tomb?

2. awoke from her flower-strewn grave to find herself beside a headless corpse?

3. impersonated the bride at a second wedding?

4. presented herself, pregnant, to the husband who thought she was dead?

5. is mourned for 16 years before being restored to her husband?

6. emerged, an abbess, after being thought drowned for some twenty years by her husband and sons?

7. survived being flung overboard in a chest?

8. survived through a head swap?

9. was reported drowned 'full fathom five'?

10. left for dead on the battlefield, rose up and fought – in his own words – 'a long hour by Shrewsbury clock'.

Answers from:

Imogen (in *Cymbeline*)

Falstaff (in *Henry IV, Part 1*)

Aemilia (in *The Comedy of Errors*)

Juliet (in *Romeo and Juliet*)

Thaisa (in *Pericles*)

Hermione (in *The Winter's Tale*)

Claudio (in *Measure for Measure*)

Alonso (in *The Tempest*)

Helena (in *All's Well that Ends Well*)

Hero (in *Much Ado About Nothing*)

ANSWERS BEGIN ON PAGE 90

Shipping News

The following headlines highlight major and minor incidents relating to shipwrecks and other incidents at sea in Shakespeare's plays. Can you match each of the following headlines to a play?

1. Pirates Rescue Problem Prince

2. Butler Saved by Barrel of Wine

3. Shipwreck off Illyria. Double Mystery

4. Bear Eats Man. Ship Lost

5. Bride-to-be Loses Brother and Dowry in Shipwreck

6. Double Twins Disaster. Shattered Mast Splits

7. Merchant Rues Third Wreck

8. No Sleep for Captain in High Seas Curse

9. Death by Walter. Duke's Past Overwhelms Him

10. Tragic Tempest Childbirth Drama

Answers from:

Pericles

Twelfth Night

The Winter's Tale

Hamlet

Henry VI, Part 2

The Tempest

Measure for Measure

The Merchant of Venice

The Comedy of Errors

Macbeth

ANSWERS BEGIN ON PAGE 92

Dreams

Which of these dreamers dreamed:

1. of 'a thousand men that fishes gnawed upon'.

2. of 'money bags'.

3. that 'my lady came and found me dead'.

4. of a statue spouting blood.

5. of three 'weird sisters'.

6. that he would never see his wife again.

7. of a 'silver basin and a ewer'.

8. a dream so beautiful that when he woke he 'cried to sleep again'.

9. of a man 'so surfeit swelled, so old and so profane'.

10. a dream that 'hath no bottom'.

Answers from:

Calpurnia (in *Julius Caesar*)

Lucullus (in *Timon of Athens*)

Banquo (in *Macbeth*)

Romeo (in *Romeo and Juliet*)

Bottom (in *A Midusmmer Night's Dream*)

Antigonus (in *The Winter's Tale*)

Clarence (in *Richard III*)

Shylock (in *The Merchant of Venice*)

Caliban (in *The Tempest*)

King Henry V/ Hal (in *Henry IV, Part 2*)

ANSWERS BEGIN ON PAGE 94

Villains

Which of these ten villains:

1. Delighted in being called 'honest'.

2. Stabbed a nurse so that she couldn't reveal a secret.

3. Raped his friend's wife.

4. Was sentenced to execution minutes after his wedding.

5. Hid in a trunk so as to spy on a woman in bed.

6. Planned to burn his brother in his own house.

7. Set his brother adrift in a boat.

8. Murdered his brother, then married the widow.

9. Was responsible for his brother being murdered and dumped in a wine barrel.

10. Stabbed himself and laid the blame on his brother.

Answers from:

Aaron (in *Titus Andronicus*)

Iago (in *Othello*)

Tarquin (in *The Rape of Lucrece*)

Antonio (in *The Tempest*)

Edmund (in *King Lear*)

Richard III (in *Richard III*)

Iachimo (in *Cymbeline*)

Oliver (in *As You Like It*)

Claudius (in *Hamlet*)

Angelo (in *Measure for Measure*)

ANSWERS BEGIN ON PAGE 96

Locations

Which play is set wholly or partially in:

1. Illyria

2. Belmont

3. Troy

4. The Forest of Arden

5. A Wood outside Athens

6. a Mediterranean brothel

7. a Gloucestershire Orchard

8. a nunnery in Vienna

9. Windsor Forest

10. the environs of a Molehill

Answers from:

ANSWERS BEGIN ON PAGE 98

The Supernatural

In which play will you find the following:

1. A Ghost who disappears when the cock crows.

2. An Apparition of 'a bloody child'.

3. 'Six personages clad in white robes, wearing on their heads garlands of bays, and golden vizards on their faces'.

4. A succession of 11 ghosts who appear to rivals on the eve of battle.

5. Fiends who shake their heads when offered blood.

6. A Harpy descending over a banquet.

7. Ghostly music on the eve of a battle.

8. A vision of Jupiter, descending on an Eagle.

9. A vanishing hind, replaced by a rose tree.

10. A report of Ghosts which did 'shriek and squeal about the streets'.

Answers from:

The Tempest

Richard III

Henry VIII

Julius Caesar

Cymbeline

Macbeth

Henry VI, Part 1

Antony and Cleopatra

Hamlet

The Two Noble Kinsmen

ANSWERS BEGIN ON PAGE 100

Fools, Clowns and Jesters

In which play is there a fool, clown or jester who:

1. finds that 'misery acquaints a man with strange bedfellows'?

2. impersonates a clergyman.

3. appears only as a skull.

4. has an argument with 'the fiend'.

5. introduces his fiancée as 'an ill favour'd thing sir, but mine own'.

6. imagines himself as the porter of hell-gate, showing 'the primrose path to the everlasting bonfire'.

7. is sent by his sister to buy spices for a feast.

8. delivers a message in a basket of pigeons.

9. delivers an instrument of death in a basket of figs.

10. inspires a king to take pity on 'houseless poverty'?

Answers from:

Titus Andronicus

Twelfth Night

King Lear

As You Like It

Hamlet

The Tempest

The Winter's Tale

The Merchant of Venice

Antony and Cleopatra

Macbeth

ANSWERS BEGIN ON
PAGE 102

The Moon in the Dream

In *A Midsummer Night's Dream*, who:

1. compares the moon to 'a step-dame, or a dowager'.

2. is pictured 'Chanting faint hymns to the cold fruitless moon'.

3. refers to the moon as 'Phoebe' beholding her 'silver visage in the watery glass'.

4. says 'ill met by moonlight'.

5. says that the 'moon looks with a watery eye'.

6. raises the problem of bringing 'moonlight into the chamber'.

7. asks 'Doth the moon shine that night we play our play?'

8. says 'This lanthorn doth the horned moon present …..'.

9. says 'I am a-weary of this moon. Would he would change'.

10. says 'Sweet Moon, I thank thee for thy sunny beams'.

Answers from:

Bottom

Hermia

Hippolyta

Lysander

Oberon

Quince

Snout

Starveling

Theseus

Titania

ANSWERS BEGIN
ON PAGE 104

'The Play's the Thing'

In 'the play scene' in *Hamlet*, who says each of the following:

1. How fares our cousin Hamlet?

2. I did enact Julius Caesar. I was kill'd 'i'th Capitol. Brutus kill'd me.

3. Nay, 'tis twice two months, my lord.

4. For us and for our tragedy,
   Here, stooping to your clemency,
   We beg your hearing patiently.

5. The instances that second marriage move
   Are base respects of thrift, but none of love.

6. For 'tis a question left us yet to prove,
   Whether love lead fortune, or else fortune love.

7. The lady doth protest too much, methinks.

8. This is one Lucianus, nephew to the king.

9. Thoughts black, hands apt, drugs fit, and time agreeing…

10. She desires to speak with you in her closet ere you go to bed.

Answers from:

Rosencrantz

Lucianus

Ophelia

Player King

Hamlet

Gertrude

Polonius

The Prologue

Player Queen

Claudius

ANSWERS
BEGIN ON
PAGE 106

New Worlds

In their different attitudes and responses, the characters below provide a richly varied image of the island world of *The Tempest*. Can you match these characters to the quotations which follow?

Gonzalo
Ferdinand
Ariel
Miranda
Sebastian
Stephano
Prospero
Caliban
Antonio
Trinculo

Who:

1. Complains: Here's neither bush nor shrub to bear off any weather at all. And another storm brewing, I hear it sing in the wind.

2. Reassures: Here is everything advantageous to life –
How lush and tasty the grass looks! How green!

3. Asserts: This island's mine, by Sycorax, my mother.

4. Wonders: This music crept by me upon the waters,
Allaying both their fury and my passion
With its sweet air.

5. Claims he heard: a hollow burst of bellowing
Like bulls, or rather lions.

6. Looks forward to being: King of the isle.

7. Calls Caliban, the island native: a plain fish, and no doubt
marketable.

8. Recalls: The strong based promontory
I have made shake, and by the spurs plucked up
The pine and cedar.

9. Sings: Where the bee sucks, there suck I,
In a cowslip's bell I lie.

10. Exclaims: Oh brave new world
That has such people in't.

ANSWERS BEGIN ON PAGE 108

The Definitive Shakespeare Quiz Book ❦ 61

ANSWERS, NOTES AND QUERIES

Answers, Notes and Queries

Note: answers are in **red** type.

THE TOP TEN

*1. To be or not to be, that is the **question**.*
This, perhaps the most famous line in all Shakespeare, expresses the world-weariness and desire for death which preoccupy **Hamlet** throughout the play.

2. All the world's a stage
*And all the men and women merely **players**.*
These words lead into the cynical **Jaques**'s vision of life as a seven act play, ending in senile oblivion.

3. Cowards die many times before their deaths,
*The **valiant** never taste of death but once.*
Is this **Julius Caesar** showing genuine heroism? Or do the lines suggest boastful arrogance? Nelson Mandela chose these lines as his favourite passage in all Shakespeare.

4. The course of true love never did run smooth.

Lysander speaks these words at the start of *A Midsummer Night's Dream*. By the end of the play it is difficult to see the teenage infatuation which he and his rival, Demetrius, feel for Hermia as 'true love'.

5. What's in a name? That which we call a rose
By any other name would smell as sweet.

Addressing the Romeo in her thoughts, Juliet has asked, 'Wherefore (why) art thou Romeo?' His name betrays him as a Montague and therefore an enemy of her family. (Interestingly, the name Romeo is now synonymous with 'lover').

6. The quality of mercy is not strain'd,
It droppeth as the gentle rain from heaven.

Does Portia's eloquent affirmation of 'mercy' square with the Christians' treatment of Shylock at the end of the *The Merchant of Venice*?

7. A horse, a horse! My kingdom for a horse!

During the battle of Bosworth Field Richard III is, momentarily, prepared to exchange his 'kingdom' for a horse. In fact, he is offered a horse and the chance to escape, but he chooses to fight on and die.

8. Shall I compare thee to a summer's day?

Though often read as a love poem, 'Sonnet 18' was probably addressed to Shakespeare's patron.

9. Is this a dagger which I see before me,
The handle toward my hand?

Macbeth sees this vision of a dagger just before he murders King Duncan. This hallucinatory moment suggests that he may be too sensitive (or too unstable) to be a successful killer.

10. O, beware, my lord, of jealousy!
It is the green-ey'd monster which doth mock
The meat it feeds on.

Iago feeds Othello with this image of jealousy. Iago is, in fact, the 'monster' who stage-manages Othello into believing that his wife, Desdemona, has been unfaithful to him.

OPENING WORDS

1. Two households, both alike in dignity,
In fair Verona, where we lay our scene.

These are the opening lines of the prologue to *Romeo and Juliet*. 'Dignity' here means 'rank' or 'social standing'.

2. Now is the winter of our discontent
Made glorious summer by this son of York.

These lines are from *Richard III*'s opening soliloquy. The 'son of York' is Richard's older brother, Edward, who has just been crowned king. There is a pun on 'son'/'sun'. The 'sun of York' contrasts with the 'winter of our discontent' – the struggle between the house of York and the house of Lancaster. Actually, Richard preferred 'the winter'.

3. If music be the food of love, play on,
Give me excess of it; that surfeiting,
*The appetite may **sicken**, and so die.*
Though *Twelfth Night* celebrates love and festivity, for most of the characters in the play 'love' is a form of sickness.

4. O for a muse of fire, that would ascend
*The brightest heaven of **invention**!*
'Invention' here means 'imagination'. Some see this opening chorus to *Henry V* as a yearning for the power of the cinema.

5. When my love swears that she is made of truth,
*I do believe her, though I know she **lies**.*
'**Sonnet 138**' painfully explores the deceptions integral to the love relationship (with the 'Dark Lady') which is at the heart of this section of the sonnet sequence.

6. When shall we three meet again?
*In thunder, lightning or in **rain**?*
Macbeth starts with an appropriately murky setting, as the three witches prepare for the meeting which will lead to Macbeth's downfall.

7. In sooth, I know not why I am so sad.

The Merchant of Venice opens with this plaintive line. Why is 'the merchant', Antonio, 'so sad'? Is it because his beloved friend, Bassanio, is planning to marry?

8. So shaken as we are, so wan with care.

Whereas Antonio's sadness is somewhat mysterious, King Henry's mood at the start of *Henry IV, Part 1* is quite understandable. Having gained the throne by an act of usurpation, he is now suffering the consequences of political instability in his kingdom.

9. Let fame, that all hunt after in their lives,
Live registered upon our brazen tombs.

Love's Labour's Lost begins and ends with reminders of death. In these opening lines, the young king of Navarre is about to attempt to persuade his three close friends to devote the next three years to study – in an attempt to achieve 'fame' and immortality. At the end of the play a messenger announces the death of the father of the Princess of France. The remainder of the play is given over to various forms of courtship.

10. Hung be the heavens with black, yield day to night!

This, the opening line of *Henry VI, Part 1*, is a truly momentous line. It leads on to an announcement of the death of the successful, but still young, King Henry V. The Wars of the Roses are about to commence. What is more, most regard this as Shakespeare's first play. His career in the theatre has started.

COURTING COUPLES

1. Beatrice: I wonder that you will still be talking Signior Benedick,
nobody marks you.
(e) Benedick: What, my dear Lady Disdain! Are you yet living?
Beatrice and Benedick in *Much Ado About Nothing*, are made for each other.
Right from the start of the play they take pleasure in mocking each other.

2. Orsino: For women are as roses, whose fair flow'r
Being once display'd, doth fall that very hour.
(h) Viola: And so they are; alas, that they are so!
To die, even when they to perfection grow!
In *Twelfth Night*, Orsino speaks to Viola without realising that 'he' is actually
a girl –or that she is in love with him. Her sad, musical reply fits her name.

3. Henry V: An angel is like you, Kate, and you are like an angel.
(a) Princess Katherine: Pardonnez moi, I cannot tell vat is 'like me'.
Princess Katherine of France is part of the peace settlement offered to Henry
V after the English victory at Agincourt. But Henry manages to make this political
proposal both charming and entertaining.

4. Petruchio: Come, come, you wasp, i' faith you are too angry.
(i) Katherina: If I be waspish, best beware my sting.
In *The Taming of the Shrew*, Petruchio thinks that Katherina, 'the shrew',
whose fortune he covets, will be easy to tame. He's wrong. Like Beatrice and
Benedick, the pair are well matched.

5. Romeo: If I profane with my unworthiest hand …..
(f) Juliet: Good pilgrim, you do wrong your hand too much …

Romeo's first words to Juliet express both his reverence and his desire. As Juliet replies, their lines intertwine to form a perfect sonnet, culminating in a kiss.

6. Cleopatra: If it be love indeed, tell me how much.
(b) Antony: There's beggary in the love that can be reckon'd.

Another legendary pair of lovers, Antony and Cleopatra's opening dialogue is shaped as a poem.

7. Diomed: What did you swear you would bestow on me?
(c) Cressida: I prithee do not hold me to mine oath.

Diomed is in the process of seducing the fickle Cressida. She has promised to give him the love token given to her by Troilus. Unknown to them, Troilus himself (and others) are watching their encounter.

8. Pyramus: O kiss me through the hole of this vile wall!
(j) Thisbe: I kiss the wall's hole, not your lips at all.

Pyramus (played by Bottom) woos Thisbe (played by Flute) in the burlesque entertainment offered at the end of the *A Midsummer Night's Dream*. 'Wall' is also an actor, so there is much scope for lewd action centring on bottoms, holes and kissing.

9. Ferdinand: My prime request,
Which I do last pronounce, is (O you wonder!)
If you be maid, or no?

*(g) **Miranda**: No wonder, sir, but certainly a maid.*

In *The Tempest*, Ferdinand and Miranda match each other for innocence and honesty – luckily, because Miranda's father Prospero is watching.

10. 'I am,' quoth he, 'expected by my friends,
And now 'tis dark, and going I shall fall'.
(d) 'In night', quoth she, 'Desire sees best of all.'

In this long narrative poem the goddess **Venus** has lured a somewhat reluctant **Adonis** away from his preferred pastime - boar-hunting with his friends.

SEX SURVEY

1. If fires be hot, knives sharp, or waters deep,
*Untied I still my virgin **knot** will keep.*

In *Pericles* **Marina**, sold to a brothel, determines to remain pure. But did she mean 'untied'? (See also answer to question 6 in the Locations quiz)

*2. Virginity breeds **mites** much like a cheese, consumes itself to the very paring, and so dies with feeding his own stomach.*

This is a small part of a lengthy diatribe against virginity in *All's Well That Ends Well*. **Parolles** would seem to be attempting to shock Helena – the play's heroine. But as the plot unfolds, we discover that Helena is set on losing her virginity to the play's cad, young Bertram.

*3. I am one, sir, that comes to tell you your daughter and the Moor are now making the beast with two **backs**.*

In *Othello*, **Iago**'s crude image of Othello (the Moor) with Desdemona is meant to unsettle Desdemona's father – which it does.

> *4. Nay, but to live*
> *In the rank sweat of an enseamed bed,*
> *Stew'd in corruption, **honeying** and making love*
> *Over the nasty sty.*

Hamlet would seem to be as troubled by his mother indulging in sex with Claudius as he is by the murder of his father.

> *5. If thou dost break her virgin knot [....] barren hate*
> *Sour-ey'd disdain, and **discord** shall bestrew*
> *The union of your bed with weeds so loathly*
> *That you shall hate it both.*

In *The Tempest,* **Prospero** is lecturing Ferdinand on the perils of pre-marital sex. Could this description of marital discord be based on Shakespeare's own over hasty-marriage to Anne Hathaway?

> *6. Me of my lawful pleasure she restrain'd,*
> *And pray'd me oft forbearance; did it with*
> *A pudency so rosy the sweet view on't*
> *Might well have warm'd old **Saturn**.*

Posthumus (Imogen's husband in *Cymbeline*) believes that his seemingly chaste wife has been unfaithful to him (see answer to question 5 in Villains quiz). Saturn, at that time the most distant of the planets, was associated with age and coldness.

7. But to the girdle do the god's inherit,
Beneath is all the fiends'.

In his madness King Lear sees sexuality as essentially evil, the work of the devil. His companions in this scene are the blind Gloucester and his son Edgar. Later Edgar will see his father's blinding as a 'just' punishment for the sexual indiscretions of his youth.

8. Give them diseases, leaving with thee their lust.
Make use of thy salt hours. Season the slaves
For tubs and baths; bring down rose-cheek'd youth
To the tub-fast and the diet.

Timon (of Athens) is urging a pair of prostitutes to spread venereal disease among their clients. Treatment for syphilis included 'sweating tubs', extreme diets and courses of mercury.

9. Th' expense of spirit in a waste of shame
Is lust in action, and till action, lust
Is perjured, murd'rous, bloody, full of blame,
Savage, extreme, rude, cruel, not to trust.

Shakespeare's passionate denunciation of lust in 'Sonnet 129' seems heartfelt. The horror of sex in Elizabethan England was linked to the advent of venereal disease in England and Europe.

10. As those that feed grow full, as blossoming time
That from the seedness the bare fallow brings

To teeming foison, even so her plenteous womb
Expresseth his full tilth and husbandry.

Elsewhere in *Measure for Measure* Lucio, who speaks these lines, sees sex as dangerous fun – a 'game of tic tac' which might result in disease, or unwanted pregnancy or both. (His friend Claudio has just been sentenced to death for fornication.) This wonderful affirmation of sex as an essentially natural, life-giving process is delivered to the chaste Isabella in a nunnery. 'Tilth' is the cultivation of ground; 'foison' is the harvest.

CREATURES GREAT AND SMALL

1. She's a beagle true-bred, and one that adores me.

In *Twelfth Night,* Sir Toby Belch says this of Maria, the romantic word 'adores' clashing comically with the unromantic image of dog-breeding.

2. It was my turquoise, I had it of Leah when I was a bachelor. I would not have given it for a wilderness of monkeys.

In *The Merchant of Venice,* this comment is made when Shylock learns that his daughter Jessica exchanged his wedding ring for a monkey. The phrase 'a wilderness of monkeys' captures both Shylock's anguish and his somewhat alien vocabulary.

3. This foul, grim and urchin-snouted boar
Whose downward eye still looketh for a grave.

In *Venus and Adonis*, the lure of the boar proves stronger than Venus's promises of amorous dalliance, but it is the boar, with his ground-snuffling snout (like an 'urchin' or hedgehog) who kills Adonis.

4. *Civil dissension is a viperous **worm***
That gnaws the bowels of the commonwealth.

This is a powerful image of the civil unrest which dominates *Henry VI, Part 1* and its sequels. The 'worm' here may also be an echo of the serpent in the Garden of Eden.

5. *I saw him run after a gilded **butterfly**, and when he caught it, he let it go again.*

In *Coriolanus,* the small child who chases the butterfly is Coriolanus's son. When he catches the butterfly, he proceeds to 'mammock' it – tear it to pieces. The Roman matrons approve.

6. *The poor **beetle** that we tread upon*
In corporal sufferance finds a pang as great
As when a giant dies.

In *Measure for Measure*, Isabella uses this image in an attempt to persuade her brother Claudio that he should not fear death. Isabella's own fear of death is insignificant in comparison to her fear of losing her virginity.

7. *There may be in the cup*
*A **spider** steep'd, and one may drink; depart*
And yet partake no venom.

In *The Winter's Tale* Leontes, his mind on the edge of madness, uses this image to argue that, like a drinker who does not see the spider at the bottom of his cup, husbands who are ignorant of their wives' adultery need not be troubled by it. Leontes says, 'I have drunk, and seen the spider'.

8. *The more you beat me, I will fawn on you.*
*Use me but as your **spaniel**; spurn me, strike me,*
Neglect me, lose me; only give me leave,
Unworthy as I am, to follow you.

In *A Midsummer Night's Dream*, Helena uses this image to express her absolute devotion to Demetrius. Not surprisingly, he runs away.

9. *Her fruit trees all unprun'd, her hedges ruin'd,*
Her knots disordered and her wholesome herbs
*Swarming with **caterpillars**.*

The under gardener who says this in *Richard II*, is comparing England under the weak King Richard to a badly- kept garden. Richard's favourite lords have earlier been called 'the caterpillars of the commonwealth'.

10. *the belching **whale***
And humming water must o'erwhelm thy corpse,
Lying with simple shells.

Despite the whale's 'belching', with this image **Pericles** evokes the strange mystery of the sea to which he has abandoned the body of his wife.

FEASTING

1. Dost thou think, because thou art virtuous, there shall be no more cakes and ale?
In *Twelfth Night* this challenge is hurled at the puritanical Malvolio, who sees feasting as dangerously immoral. 'Cakes and ale' represent pleasurable indulgence.

2. The Justice
In fair round belly with good capon lined.
The Justice here represents the fifth Act of the seven Ages of Man in Jacques's speech, 'All the world's a stage' in *As You Like It*. Dining on fine plump poultry would emphasise the man's social and physical well-being.

3. When roasted crabs hiss in the bowl
Then nightly sings the staring owl.
Crabs are actually crab apples. Here they help to summon up the season of Winter in the song which concludes *Love's Labour's Lost*, 'When icicles hang by the wall'.

4. Feed him with apricocks and dewberries,
With purple grapes, green figs and mulberries.
In *A Midsummer Night's Dream*, Titania is ordering a feast of fruit for her captive lover. But since Bottom has been turned into an ass, what he actually wants is oats and hay.

5. We have hot venison-pasty to dinner; come, gentlemen, I hope we shall drink down all unkindness.

Master Page, in *The Merry Wives of Windsor*, is hoping that this dinner will mend a squabble between Falstaff and Shallow.

6. Good thou, save me a piece of marchpane; and, as thou lov'st me, let the porter let in Susan Grindstone and Nell.

In *Romeo and Juliet*, marchpane (or marzipan) is being served at the Capulet Ball. The speaker, a servant, is rushing to clear away the banquet ready for the dancing. He looks forward to relaxing with girlfriends when it's all over.

7. I know a wench married in an afternoon as she went to the garden for parsley to stuff a rabbit.

This is a throwaway line in *The Taming of the Shrew*, suggesting that a girl can be seduced ('married') in a casual instant. This is another servant's eye view of Elizabethan feasting.

8. Eight wild-boars roasted whole at a breakfast and but twelve persons there! Is't true?

In *Antony and Cleopatra*, this example of conspicuous consumption is one of the rumours about life in Egypt at Cleopatra's court. The Roman who quotes it is caught between wonder and disapproval.

9. The funeral baked-meats did coldly furnish forth the marriage table.

This sardonic comment is typical of Hamlet's scorn and disgust at his mother's 'o'er hasty' move from widowhood to re-marriage.

*10. O but a half-penny'orth of **bread** to this intolerable deal of sack!*

In *Henry IV, Part 1*, Prince Hal is rifling through the pockets of his totally drunk friend, Falstaff. A pub receipt, itemising repeated orders of 'sack' (drink) ends with a single order of bread – aptly summarising Falstaff's priorities.

'WHAT'S IN A NAME?'

1. Malvolio means **ill-will**. In *Twelfth Night* he is the enemy of festivity and his last words, 'I'll be reveng'd on the whole pack of you', leave him a threatening outsider to the world of comedy.

2. Fortinbras, the 'victor' in *Hamlet,* has a name which means **arm of iron**. He is a man of action in marked contrast to Hamlet, whose introspection inhibits action.

3. Doll Tearsheet, the whore in *Henry IV, Part 2*, has a name which suggests that she is (or has been) **sexually very active**!

4. Bottom, a weaver, is at the **lower end of the social scale**. There may also be an intended pun on **Bottom/Arse/Ass** – though some etymologists argue that the word 'bottom' was not used as a synonym for 'bum' until well into the 18th century. However, *A Midsummer Night's Dream* is consciously patterned with Theseus, the 'philosopher king' representing 'the head', the lovers representing 'the heart' and the artisan play-makers representing 'the nether regions'. Shakespeare seems to have been ahead of his time!

5. The name of Cordelia, Lear's youngest daughter, plays on the idea of **a cordial** (a restorative for **the heart**). It is Cordelia who restores Lear to sanity after his heart has been broken. Interestingly, however, shortly before Shakespeare wrote *King Lear* there was a court case which might well have influenced him. An elderly gentlemen, Sir Brian Annesley, was declared insane by his two older daughters who hoped to inherit his property. They were challenged by his youngest daughter – whose name was Cordell.

6. Hotspur is the nick-name of Henry Percy in *Henry IV, Part 1*. The name suggests that **he rides impulsively** into battle – spurring his horse with **anger or passion**. His hot-headedness leads eventually to his death at the hands of his more level-headed rival, Prince Henry, (known as 'Hal' and later to become King Henry V).

7. The name Ajax plays with the word 'jakes' – a vulgar term for a **lavatory**. Shakespeare makes good use of this association when, in *Troilus and Cressida*, Ajax is selected by the Greeks to fight the Trojan champion, Hector. When the scurrilous wit, Thersites, says 'Ajax goes up and down the field, asking for himself' we miss the humour if we don't see that Thersites means that Ajax is so scared that he is desperate to find 'a jakes' – to relieve himself!

8. Crab, in *The Two Gentlemen of Verona* is a dog. He is nothing but trouble for his devoted master, Launce, and is particularly well named. The word crab was an abbreviation of '**crab-apple**'. Like the crab-apple, Launce's dog is **sour** and ungenerous.

9. Parolles in *All's Well that Ends Well*, is an empty braggart. His name, meaning 'words', suggests that he is all mouth and no substance.

10. Abhorson in *Measure for Measure* is the executioner. Though he expresses contempt for the profession of Pompey, the bawd, his own name means 'son of a whore'. There is also a pun on 'abhor' – meaning to horrify or disgust.

CURSES AND INSULTS

1. God hath given you one face, and you make yourselves another. You jig and amble and you lisp, you nickname God's creatures and make your wantonness your ignorance.

Hamlet says this to Ophelia, but he is expressing his disgust for women in general. Women's make-up – in an age where many faces were pock-marked – was a popular theme for satirists.

2. You are pictures out of doors,
Bells in your parlours, wild-cats in your kitchens,
Saints in your injuries, devils being offended,
Players in your housewifery, housewives in your beds.

Here Iago, in *Othello*, is joking with Desdemona and his own wife, Emilia. The idea of women being 'pictures out of doors', echoes Hamlet's jibe about 'painting' 'Bells' implies that women's tongues keep gossiping like clappers. The last line suggests a comically topsy-turvy world, where women play at being careful housewives but are niggardly in bed.

3. If he were open'd and you find so much blood in his liver as will clog the foot of a flea, I'll eat the rest of the anatomy.

Sir Toby Belch in *Twelfth Night* is sneering at Sir Andrew Aguecheek's lack of courage.

4. Some report a sea-maid spawn'd him; some that he was begot between two stock-fishes. But it is certain that when he makes water, his urine is congealed ice.

In *Measure for Measure*, **Lucio** revels in slander. His comment here on Angelo seems appropriate at the time. We later discover that Angelo is a study in repressed sexuality.

5. Have you not a moist eye, a dry hand, a yellow cheek, a white beard, a decreasing leg, an increasing belly? Is not your voice broken, your wind short, your chin double, your wit single, and every part about you blasted with antiquity.

This is the **Chief Justice** in *Henry IV, Part 2* mocking Falstaff who has been behaving like an irresponsible young man.

6. That bottled spider, that foul bunch'd back toad.

Queen Elizabeth says this of her brother-in-law, the hunch-backed Richard III shortly after he has murdered her two young sons – but before she has granted him permission to marry her daughter! Both 'bottled' and 'bunch'd back' refer to Richard's swollen, deformed body.

7. You common cry of curs, whose breath I hate
As reek o' the rotten fens, whose loves I prize

As the dead carcasses of unburied men
That do corrupt my air.

Coriolanus is hurling abuse at the Roman plebeians who have rejected him. The word 'corrupt' completes the strong alliterative pattern of the passage.

8. Into her womb convey sterility.
Dry up in her the organs of increase,
And from her derogate body, never spring
A babe to honour her!

King Lear's terrible curse seems to make a monster out of his daughter Goneril. ('Derogate' means debased or degenerate.) Until this moment her behaviour could be regarded as 'reasonable'.

9. Son of sixteen,
Pluck the lined crutch from thy old limping sire,
With it beat out his brains.

Timon starts out as a generous patron, giving money and gifts to his sycophantic friends. When he discovers that their friendship has been dependent on his wealth, he becomes even more generous in his abuse. His anarchic cursing is levelled at all humanity. (Here 'lined' means padded.)

10. Now the rotten diseases of the south, the guts-griping ruptures, catarrhs, loads a' gravel in the back, lethargies, cold palsies, raw eyes, dirt-rotten livers, whissing lungs bladders full of imposthume, sciaticas, lime kilns i' th' palm, incurable bone-ache, and the rivell'd fee-simple of the tetter, take and take again such preposterous discoveries.

Thersites, in *Troilus and Cressida*, is the most vitriolic of all Shakespeare's characters. Here he is detailing the symptoms of venereal disease – almost wishing it to break out in both the Greek and the Roman camps. 'Whissing' here means 'wheezing'; 'imposthume' means 'ulceration' and the 'rivell'd fee-simple of the tetter' can be paraphrased loosely as 'the perpetual inheritance of itching'.

SIMILES

1. See, see King Richard doth himself appear,
As doth the blushing discontented sun
From out the fiery portals of the east.

Richard II is about to be deposed. As rightful king of England, the comparison to the sun is appropriate – though unexpected coming from Henry Bolingbroke, the usurper. In the Elizabethan World Picture, associations were repeatedly made between the King and the sun.

2. By being seldom seen, I could not stir
But like a comet I was wondered at.

These lines are from *Henry IV, Part 1*. By comparing himself to a 'comet', Henry IV (formerly Bolingbroke) reminds us that he gained the throne through an act of usurpation.

3. The poor condemned English,
Like sacrifices, by their watchful fires
Sit patiently and inly ruminate.

With this image, the Chorus in *Henry V* conjures the mood of the English camp on the night before the battle of Agincourt. Weakened by disease and hopelessly outnumbered, they are expecting to be heavily defeated.

4. And pity, like a naked new-born babe
Striding the blast, or heaven's cherubin, hors'd
Upon the sightless couriers of the air,
Shall blow the horrid deed in every eye,
That tears shall drown the wind.

Macbeth's apocalyptic image of the heavens in anguish at the idea of Duncan's murder, centres on the 'naked new born babe' as a concrete image of 'pity'.

5. For time is like a fashionable **host**
That slightly shakes his parting guest by th' hand,
And with his arms outstretched as he would fly
Grasps in the comer.

In *Troilus and Cressida,* Ulysses's comparison helps stir Achilles – desirous of fame and immortality – into action. The play abounds with images of Time as the great destroyer – a nice irony since Shakespeare is dealing with the fall of Troy, a mythical subject which has transcended time.

6. He doth bestride the narrow world
Like a Colossus, and we petty men
Walk under his huge legs, and peep about
To find ourselves dishonourable graves.

This image of Julius Caesar's great stature is undermined by the sneering Cassius. He depicts himself and other ordinary mortals as they 'peep' through the statue's great legs. The alternative to finding 'dishonourable graves' is to pull down the Colossus – in other words, to murder Caesar.

7. *As flies to wanton boys are we to th' gods,*
They kill us for their sport.

Gloucester's brutal image, in *King Lear*, of deities playing wantonly with human lives is echoed in William Blake's 'Auguries of Innocence' - 'The wanton boy who kills the fly/ Shall feel the spider's enmity'.

8. *On her left breast*
A mole cinque-spotted, like the crimson drops
I' th' bottom of a cowslip.

This image from *Cymbeline,* of a mole on the breast of the heroine, Imogen, is Shakespeare's most intimate close-up. Momentarily the villain Iachimo takes on the persona of an evil fairy. (The word 'cinque' means five.)

9. *She looks like sleep,*
As she would catch another Antony
In her strong toil of grace.

In *Antony and Cleopatra* this generous and beautiful tribute to dead Cleopatra, seeming to establish her for an eternity of grace, is spoken by the generally austere Augustus Caesar.

10. Our natures do pursue,
Like **rats** *that ravin down their proper bane,*
A thirsty evil; and when we drink we die.

In ***Measure for Measure*** the condemned Claudio compares the lust which has led to his death sentence to the thirst which drives a rat poisoned with ratsbane to drink water and in so doing die.

DYING WORDS

1. Mount, mount, my soul, my seat is up on high;
Whilst my gross **flesh** *sinks downward, here to die.*

As an anointed king, murdered on the order of his usurper, **Richard II** seems confident of going to a better place.

2. Now am I dead,
Now am I fled;
My soul is in the **sky**.

These are the dying words of **Pyramus/Bottom** in the play performed at the end of *A Midsummer Night's Dream.* Is this an intentional parody of Richard II's death?

3. I am a scribbled form drawn with a pen
Upon a parchment, and against this fire
Do I **shrink** *up.*

King John is poisoned by a monk (actually a suicide-poisoner, because his job

as royal taster means that he dies of the same poison, burning up from within).
'Shrink' gives the idea of being shrivelled up by the heat.

4. Pray you undo this button. Thank you, sir.
*Do you see this? Look on her. Look, her **lips**,*
Look there, look there!
Are we meant to believe that **Lear**'s heart 'bursts smilingly' as he dies believing
that Cordelia is still alive?

5. Ask for me tomorrow, and you shall find
*me a **grave** man.*
Mercutio, in *Romeo and Juliet*, fatally wounded in a street fight, dies, as he has
lived – wittily.

6. Dost thou not see my baby at my breast,
*That **sucks** the nurse asleep?*
Legend has it that **Cleopatra** studied ways of dying. Her choice of the asp
(which she calls her 'baby') enables her to die with controlled dignity.

*7. I took by the throat th'uncircumcised **dog***
And slew him, thus!
Othello dies as he has lived – theatrically. Othello's friends, realising that he
is suicidal, think they have disarmed him. But Othello gives his own epitaph,
concluding with an instance of his fighting for the Venetians against their Turkish
enemy, and on the word 'thus!' produces a hidden sword.

8. O, I could prophesy,
But that the icy and cold hand of death
Lies on my tongue.

Hotspur, in *Henry IV, Part 1*, has in life epitomised energy and eloquence (see answer to question 6 in the 'What's in a Name?' quiz).

9. I, that never feared any, am vanquished by famine,
not by valour.

Abandoned by his followers, **Jack Cade**, the rebel leader in *Henry VI, Part 2*, is finally cornered in a garden, desperate to find food. His main concern is that people might think that he was beaten by a courage superior to his.

10. The rest is silence.

Given that **Hamlet** speaks more words than almost anyone in Shakespeare, his last words are surprisingly brief.

RESURRECTIONS

1. In *Romeo and Juliet* Juliet's 'death' is staged by the Friar. Before taking his potion, she imagined the horror of her awakening in the Capulet tomb – but it didn't include finding the body of Romeo dead beside her.

2. Like Juliet, Imogen in *Cymbeline* has taken a drug which leaves her seeming dead. Like Juliet, she wakes to find a dead body beside her. But this body is headless and, though it is dressed in her husband's clothes, it isn't her husband.

3. In *Much Ado About Nothing* Claudio, believing that he has caused **Hero**'s death by slandering her at the altar, readily agrees to marry her cousin instead. But Hero has only feigned death and appears at the altar a second time herself. The audience are left wondering whether Claudio deserves his second chance to marry the woman he loves.

4. In *All's Well That Ends Well* Bertram, like Claudio, believes that his wife **Helena** is dead and readily agrees to marry another in her place. Since Helena first trapped him into a reluctant unconsummated marriage and later trapped him into sleeping with her, when she arrives to claim her husband all may not be as well as the play's title suggests.

5. In contrast to the feigned death and immediate marriage in *Much Ado*, **Hermione**'s feigned death in *The Winter's Tale* is kept a secret for sixteen years. When she is re-united with her husband, Leontes, the audience shares his impression that a miracle has occurred and senses that he has deserved his second chance.

6. In *The Comedy of Errors* **Aemilia** is thought to have drowned some twenty three years before the opening scene of the play. At the end of the play, she is discovered by her husband and sons to be alive and well and living as the abbess of a nearby convent in Ephesus.

7. Some 15 to 20 years after writing *The Comedy of Errors*, Shakespeare replayed Aemilia's story much more dramatically in *Pericles*. **Thaisa**, thought to

be dead, is thrown overboard during a storm. Luckily she is rescued and revived. She becomes a high priestess at the Temple of Diana where many years later she is re-united with her husband and daughter. Again the reunion takes place in Ephesus.

8. In *Measure for Measure* Angelo gives instructions that he be brought the head of **Claudio**, sentenced to death for fornication. After the intervention of Providence and some hasty last minute planning, Angelo is presented with the head of a prisoner not unlike Claudio who happens to die just in time.

9. In *The Tempest* **Alonso** dies symbolically. His son, Ferdinand, hears of the drowning through Ariel's magical song ('Full fathom five thy father lies'). But Alonso has been preserved and undergoes a regeneration hinted at in the song – 'Nothing of him that doth fade, / But doth suffer a sea-change,/ Into something rich and strange'.

10. In *King Henry IV, Part 1* **Falstaff** survives the battle of Shrewsbury by feigning death, reckoning that 'the better part of valour is discretion'. Dismissed as dead by Hal, Falstaff rises, and later claims that he, not Hal, killed Hotspur after having fought with him for an hour.

SHIPPING NEWS

1. **Hamlet** has been sent abroad with the intention that he will be executed on arrival in England. However, Pirates attack the ship, enabling him to escape and – eventually – to revenge his father's murder.

2. In *The Tempest* the King's butler, Stephano, survives 'the tempest' and resulting shipwreck by floating to shore on a barrel of wine. From the moment of his arrival to the end of the play, he and his associates get more and more drunk.

3. In *Twelfth Night* the twins, Viola and Sebastian, both survive shipwreck. Each thinks that the other is drowned. Their separate arrivals in Illyria cause emotional havoc.

4. In *The Winter's Tale* Antigonus is given the unlucky task of abandoning the baby Perdita on the shores of Bohemia. His death is preceded by the strangest of all Shakespeare's stage directions: 'Exit pursued by a bear'. Would this have been a real bear from the nearby bear gardens?

5. In *Measure for Measure* , we learn that before the action begins, Mariana, betrothed to Angelo, lost her dowry when her brother's ship was wrecked at at sea. As a result Angelo (only 'angel on the outward side') abandoned her, leaving her lonely and disgraced.

6. *The Comedy of Errors* begins with old Egeon telling how, following a shipwreck, he and his wife with their baby twin sons and their twin slaves attached themselves to the ship's mast. Shortly before being rescued, the mast struck a great rock and was split in two, leaving the family divided.

7. In *The Merchant of Venice* Antonio, the merchant of Venice, guarantees Shylock's loan of money to his beloved Bassanio. The loss of ships and cargo, places Antonio's life in forfeit.

8. A trick question, this. Whereas the other incidents at sea affect the central characters in the plays, this shipwreck in *Macbeth* is much more incidental. Shortly before meeting with Macbeth, one of the witches tells of how, having been refused 'chestnuts' by 'a sailor's wife', she is planning to take revenge by wrecking the husband's ship.

9. Another trick question – allowing for the latitude of journalistic puns and/ or misprints. In *Henry VI, Part 2,* the Duke of Suffolk, having organised the murder of the good Duke Humphrey, flees from England. On board ship he is recognised by a seaman called 'Walter' – and an old prophecy, that he would be killed by someone called Walter, is fulfilled.

10. Thaisa, wife of **Pericles**, appears to die in childbirth during a storm at sea. To appease the superstitious seamen, who believe that carrying a dead body is unlucky, she is thrown overboard (see the answer to question 7 in the Resurrections quiz).

DREAMS

1. **Clarence** in *Richard III* recounts his vivid nightmare of drowning shortly before he is murdered.

2. **Shylock** in *The Merchant of Venice* ignores his dream of 'money bags' and leaves his house in the care of his daughter - who promptly elopes, taking with her much of his wealth.

3. **Romeo** in *Romeo and Juliet* wakes refreshed from a dream which ended with Juliet reviving him with kisses. Tragically the dream is only partly prophetic.

4. **Calpurnia** in *Julius Caesar* tells Caesar of her dream. He is flattered to accept a conspirator's interpretation, that the dream should be read as an image of himself providing life blood to the nation. But the dream has frightened Calpurnia and like the other omens (see answer to question 10 in the Supernatural quiz) proves prophetic. A few hours later her husband's assassins will bathe their hands in his blood.

5. **Banquo**'s dream (which he tells to Macbeth) shows that he is haunted by the witches whom he had earlier dismissed as 'instruments of darkness'. Their prophecy, that his line will reign in Scotland, proves to be true. King James, for whom the play was written, believed in witches and regarded himself as a descendent of Banquo.

6. In *The Winter's Tale* **Antigonus** recounts a dream in which he was visited by Hermione, asked to name the infant he is abandoning 'Perdita', and warned that he will never see his wife again. The dream proves to be prophetic.

7. In *Timon of Athens* **Lucullus**, one of Timon's flatterers, interprets his dream to mean that he is about to be showered with presents. The dishes appear at Timon's final feast but are uncovered to reveal nothing but warm water. First the contents, then the dishes are thrown at the sycophantic guests who are driven out.

8. In *The Tempest* **Caliban** compares the music which he hears in his dreams to a glimpse of heaven.

9. In *King Henry IV, Part 2* **Hal** has spent his formative years in Falstaff's company. Emerging as the newly crowned **Henry V** he now dismisses Falstaff and his youth as a 'bad dream'. With the words 'I know thee not old man, Fall to thy prayers', Falstaff, together with his world of humour and sensual indulgence is rejected.

10. In *A Midsummer Night's Dream* **Bottom** can only accept his transformation into an ass if he thinks of it as a dream. The alternative is too embarrassing to contemplate!

VILLAINS

1. **Iago**'s reputation as a good, honest, straight-talking fellow, places him beyond suspicion and helps him to destroy Othello. He shows no remorse for his wickedness and has been seen by critics as the incarnation of evil.

2. **Aaron** in *Titus Andronicus* is Shakespeare's first study in absolute evil. Having revelled in murder, mutilation and seduction, he declares at the end of the play:

> *If one good deed in all my life I did,*
> *I do repent it from my very soul.*

In fact, shortly before this boast, he has saved the life of his infant son – a deed which might trouble him in Hell!

3. In *The Rape of Lucrece* **Tarquin**, fired by Lucrece's beauty and chaste reputation, takes advantage of her husband's absence and rapes her. She then kills herself. Later Shakespeare revisits the moment as, setting the scene for the murder of Duncan, Macbeth conjures an image of 'wither'd Murder' moving 'with Tarquin's ravishing strides' towards his victim.

4. In *Measure for Measure* **Angelo**, though sentenced to death as a would-be murderer and 'virgin violator', is reprieved at the end of the play following Isabella's plea for mercy.

5. In *Cymbeline* **Iachimo**, having gained access to Imogen's bed chamber, easily persuades her husband Posthumous that she has been unfaithful. By the end of the play, Iachimo repents and is saved.

6. In *As You Like It* **Oliver** begins the play as one of two evil brothers (the other is Duke Frederick, the young usurper). Oliver ends the play repenting and falling in love.

7. In *The Tempest* Prospero manages to effect the conversion of King Alonso. However, his own brother **Antonio** – the usurper who cast him adrift - is unrepentant, remaining a sneering cynic, quite unmoved by the wonders of the island.

8. Described by Hamlet at the end of the play as an 'incestuous, murd'rous, damned Dane' **Claudius** is a villain in the Machiavellian tradition –he will do

anything to gain and retain political power. Was marrying his brother's sister incestuous? The books of Leviticus and Deuteronomy take opposite viewpoints.

9. **Richard III** is particularly calculating and cruel in arranging the murder of his brother Clarence.

10. In *King Lear* **Edmund,** moments before his death, repents and endeavours (in vain) to save the lives of Lear and Cordelia. Readers will have noticed that the last five of the villains in this section all practise their villainy on younger or older brothers. This 'Cain and Abel' motif clearly interested Shakespeare. Shakespeare, himself, had a younger brother who followed him to London and became an actor. His name? Edmund.

LOCATIONS

1. In the second scene of *Twelfth Night* much is made of the setting in the opening exchange:

> *Viola: What country friends is this?*
> *Captain: This is Illyria lady.*
> *Viola: And what should I do in Illyria?*
> *My brother, he is in Elysium.*

And so Illyria, with its near echo of the word delirium, is associated with Elysium – the land of the happy dead – assisting to create the strange world marked by mourning, madness, festivity and love.

2. In *The Merchant of Venice* the scenes set in magical Belmont, where suitors have to pass a Casket test and where music and the harmony of the heavens are accompaniments to discourses on love, provide a contrast to the mercantile, racially riven Venice.

3. 'In Troy, there lies the scene' says the Prologue. The sad story of *Troilus and Cressida* takes centre stage, though we are never allowed to forget the love story of Paris and Helen which led to the legendary war and which provides a backdrop for their tragedy.

4. In *As You Like It* the Forest of Arden offers a world of nature in contrast to the sophistications of court life. Shakespeare enjoys but also satirises the conventions of Arcadian romance.

5. *A Midsummer Night's Dream* starts and ends in Athens. This is not just another 'mediterranean setting'. Athens is the birthplace of western philosophy. Theseus who rules the Athenian court is a 'philosopher king' who advocates the superiority of reason. The Wood outside Athens sets up a contrast between 'reason' and its opposites: love, imagination and madness.

6. In *Pericles* the young heroine Marina is sold to a brothel keeper in Mytilene. In no time her purity has converted the customers to following the path of virtue.

7. In *Henry IV, Part 2* Falstaff, recruiting men for his batallion, visits an old acquaintance, Justice Shallow, who owns an estate in Gloucestershire. The visit

enables Shakespeare to provide a wonderfully detailed picture of a country backwater – far from the riot and rebellion of the main plot.

8. In *Measure for Measure* the nunnery offers Isabella an escape from the sexual excess which characterises the many 'dark corners' of Vienna – with its brothels, its shady streets and its prison. The 'votarists of Saint Clare' were renowned for the austerity of their order. We hear sister Francisca instructing Isabella in the rules she will have to obey when she has made her vows. The flatness of the language is in marked contrast to the energetic affirmation of life provided by Lucio. (See answer to question 10 in the Sex Survey quiz).

9. The climax of this 'city comedy', *The Merry Wives of Windsor,* occurs in Windsor Forest, where Falstaff impersonates the ghost of Herne the Hunter in a final attempt to seduce the 'merry wives'.

10. On the Elizabethan stage the 'molehill' would have been a simple stage block, probably the same stage block on which the king's throne was placed. On both occasions that a 'molehill' is specifed in *Henry VI, Part 3*, it is used ironically to emphasise the contrast between glory and ignominy.

THE SUPERNATURAL

1. In *Hamlet* when the cock crows the Ghost of Hamlet's father starts 'like a guilty thing upon a fearful summons'. This implied fear of daylight suggests that the Ghost might be an evil spirit, perhaps come to lure Hamlet to damnation. But

when the Ghost speaks, it gives the impression of being a genuine spirit suffering in purgatory.

2. In *Macbeth* the second apparition conjured from the Witches' cauldron can later be identified as a baby 'from his mother's womb untimely ripp'd' (born by Caesarian section). It is this baby, grown into the avenging figure of Macduff, who explodes Macbeth's sense of his invulnerability. Babes, bloody or otherwise, are a feature of the play's verbal and visual imagery (see answer to question 4 in the Similes quiz). The small children of Macduff are brutally murdered and earlier Lady Macbeth boasts that she is capable of 'dashing the brains out' of her own suckling infant.

3. In *Henry VIII* the dying Katherine of Aragon (the first of Henry's six wives) is granted this vision of 'spirits of peace' before she dies.

4. **Richard III** has been responsible for the deaths of all the eleven ghosts who appear to him and to his rival, Richmond, on the eve of the Battle of Bosworth Field.

5. In *Henry VI, Part 1* Joan of Arc is shown to be a witch trafficking with demons. Elsewhere in the play she is treated more sympathetically.

6. In *The Tempest* Ariel, in the form of a harpy, confronts the 'three men of sin' (Antonio, Sebastian and Alonso) at the very moment they were about to enjoy a magical banquet.

7. In *Antony and Cleopatra* music is heard before Antony's last battle. The soldiers interpret it as a sign that the great god Hercules is leaving him.

8. In *Cymbeline* Jupiter, King of the Roman Gods, descends in 'thunder and lightning' to bring comfort to Posthumus who is languishing in prison.

9. In *The Two Noble Kinsmen* Emilia, loved by Palamon and Arcite (the two kinsmen who are about to fight for her), visits the altar of Diana in the hope that the Goddess will either assist her in ensuring that the best man wins or else retain her as a vestal virgin. After the hind which she has brought as an offering vanishes and is replaced by a rose tree with a single rose, there is 'a sudden twang of instruments' as the rose falls, a sign that Diana has released her.

10. In *Julius Caesar* Caesar's wife, Calpurnia, relates this (among several other portents) in an attempt to prevent Caesar from going to the Capitol. He ignores the portents and is assassinated. The idea of ghosts shrieking and squealing is repeated in *Hamlet* when Horatio tells of how when 'the mightiest Julius fell,/ The graves stood tenanted and the sheeted dead/ Did squeak and gibber in the Roman streets.'

FOOLS, CLOWNS AND JESTERS

1. In *The Tempest* Trinculo, Jester to King Alonso, takes refuge from the storm by hiding under Caliban's gaberdine. Together they are mistaken for a two-headed monster by the drunken butler, Stephano.

2. In *Twelfth Night* Feste, the lady Olivia's fool, stars in the hilarious but cruel baiting of Malvolio by pretending to be a clergyman come to cure him of his lunacy.

3. In *Hamlet* Yorick, the late king Hamlet's jester, has been dead for more than twenty years when his skull is unearthed. It provokes both nostalgia and disgust, leading into Hamlet's celebrated meditation on mortality.

4. In *The Merchant of Venice* the clown, Launcelot Gobbo, wants to leave his Scrooge-like master, Shylock, and stages a comic monologue in which he impersonates both 'the fiend' – tempting him to work for the glamorous young Bassanio – and his conscience. The fiend wins.

5. In *As You Like It* Touchstone, the court fool, proves somewhat unsophisticated in his choice of a mate. Audrey, the goatherd, suits him in spite of being a 'foul slut'.

6. In *Macbeth* the role of the Porter, offering the potential for topical ad-libbing, would have gone to one of the regular clowns in the theatre company. (Alexander Pope, in his 18th century edition, cut the whole Porter scene, believing that none of it could have been written by Shakespeare.)

7. In *The Winter's Tale* Perdita's adopted brother, described in the dramatis personae as 'a clown', is the butt of much humour - most hilariously when, sent to buy spices for the sheep-shearing feast, he is robbed by the rogue Autolycus.

8. In *Titus Andronicus* this clown, amiably agreeing to carry a message from Titus to the Emperor, receives a death sentence for his pains.

9. In *Antony and Cleopatra* the Clown brings Cleopatra a basket of figs containing the asps that will kill her. Though described as a 'simple country fellow' he seems to be a cryptic representation of death itself, delivering Cleopatra's fate as a kind of blessing: 'I wish you joy o' th' worm!'

10. In *King Lear* Shakespeare made fullest dramatic use of the fool figure. Lear's Fool is part conscience, part shrewd adviser and part representative of all who suffer from the corruptions of society.

THE MOON IN THE DREAM

1. **Theseus** in his opening speech announces that he and Hippolyta must wait until the new moon before they can marry. He compares the current moon to an elderly chaperone who prevents them from fulfilling their desires.

2. **Hermia** is told by Theseus that if she disobeys her father (who wants her to marry Demetrius and not Lysander) she will have to choose between death and the nunnery. Again, the moon (cold and fruitless) is pictured as the enemy to sexuality.

3. **Lysander** is something of a poet according to Hermia's father, who suggests that he has 'bewitch'd' Hermia by giving her 'rhymes'. This image of the moon in water, hints at Lysander's poetic potential.

4. **Oberon** greets his wife, the fairy queen with the words 'Ill met by moonlight, proud Titania'. The two are quarrelling over the possession of a changeling child.

5. **Titania** the victim of Oberon's spell, falls passionately in love with Bottom, who has just been transformed into an ass. The chaste moon's eye is 'watery' because she and the flowers of the forest are about to weep: they weep when chastity is violated. Bottom, the ass, is about to be 'raped' by Titania.

6. **Quince**, the director of 'Pyramus and Thisbe', which includes a crucial night-time scene, raises the problem. In this scene Shakespeare is satirising amateur attempts at achieving stage realism.

7. **Snout** asks the question. On establishing that the moon will shine on the night of their performance, Bottom suggests that the company should arrange to leave a window open to let in real moonshine as an accompaniment to their 'very tragical mirth'. Quince has a better idea, that 'one must come in with a bush of thorns and a lanthorn, and say that he comes to disfigure or present the person of moonshine'.

8. **Starveling** is chosen to 'disfigure' the moon.

9. **Hippolyta**, like other members of the court audience, is hard on poor Starveling. They interrupt him repeatedly so that he cannot get beyond his opening couplet, and retires in a huff: 'All that I have to say is to tell you that the

lanthorn is the moon, I the man 'i 'th moon, this thorn-bush my thorn bush, and this dog my dog.'

10. **Bottom**, as Pyramus. The line is characteristic of the quality of the text of 'Pyramus and Thisbe'.

'THE PLAY'S THE THING'

1. **Claudius** means to ask Hamlet how he is, but Hamlet – his brain working furiously – makes a pun on the word 'fares', taking it to mean 'feeds'. His response shows a dazzling word play, bordering, perhaps, on insanity:

Excellent, i' faith, of the chameleon's dish, I eat the air,
promise-cramm'd – you cannot feed capons so.

Chameleons were thought to eat air. Hamlet makes a pun on 'air' /'heir'. Capons were stuffed with food to prepare them for the table. So Hamlet's answer can be decoded to mean: 'I distrust your promise that I shall be your heir and I suspect you are planning to have me killed.' Does Claudius understand Hamlet's message, or is he - like most of the audience – bewildered? (Soon after this scene, Claudius sends Hamlet to England instructing the English king to have him killed.)

2. **Polonius**. This is another passage rich in meaning. Shakespeare wrote *Julius Caesar* shortly before *Hamlet*. Almost certainly, the roles of Brutus and Hamlet would have been taken by the company's star actor, Richard Burbage and quite probably the actor who played Julius Caesar would have been playing Polonius.

So Polonius's anecdote about being killed by Brutus/Burbage takes on a sinister irony when in the very next scene, Hamlet/Burbage kills him again.

3. **Ophelia**. Hamlet, prone to exaggeration, has just said to Ophelia, 'look how cheerfully my mother looks, and my father died within's two hours'. Ophelia's response ''tis twice two months' triggers a sarcastic tirade against the shortness of mourning and memory.

4. **The Prologue**. When Ophelia, trying hard to please Hamlet, comments that the Prologue is 'brief', Hamlet bitterly replies 'As woman's love'.

5. **The Player Queen**. Quite possibly Hamlet wrote these lines himself.

6. **The Player King**. Again, these may be lines written by Hamlet to embarrass his mother.

7. **Gertrude** is riled by the Player Queen speaking at length about the suspect motives of widows who remarry.

8. **Hamlet**. This is one of the most enigmatic lines in the play. Why does Hamlet tell the assembled audience that Lucianus, the murderer, is 'nephew to the king'? Claudius was of course brother, not nephew, to the late king Hamlet. Is the phrase 'nephew to the king' intentional or accidental? Could it be Hamlet subconsciously playing out an Oedipus role?

9. **Lucianus**'s short speech leads to Claudius calling for 'lights' and the abandoning of the play. Are we meant to think that only Hamlet and Horatio see this as a guilty response? Do the remainder of the court see Claudius's behaviour as an appropriate admonishment to a mad 'nephew'?

10. **Rosencrantz**. But it might well have been Guildenstern, the two acting as one. Though Hamlet initiates the play scene in an attempt to 'catch the conscience of the King' and arranges to write a few passages to add to the text of 'The Murder of Gonzago', throughout the scene he seems as eager to 'catch the conscience' of his mother as he is to catch his uncle. He chooses to go to his mother now, missing an opportunity to kill Claudius on the way.

NEW WORLDS

1. Of all those shipwrecked on the island, **Trinculo**, Alonso's jester is the most timorous and finds the island inhospitable and threatening.

2. The old counsellor, **Gonzalo**, partly in an attempt to cheer up Alonso (mourning for the loss of Ferdinand) tries to see the island as a potential utopia.

3. **Caliban**, having been born on the island, has been enslaved by Prospero whom he resents as a usurper.

4. Believing that he is the sole survivor of the wreck, Prince **Ferdinand** sits on a bank, mourning the death of his father, Alonso. Ariel's music leads him towards Miranda.

5. **Sebastian**, envious and weak, agrees to a plot to stab his brother, King Alonso. When the sleeping Alonso is magically alerted, this threat of wild animals is Sebastian's excuse for being found with his sword suspiciously drawn.

6. **Stephano**, Alonso's butler, persuades Trinculo and Caliban (corrupted by Stephano's alcohol) to join him in a murderous coup against Prospero.

7. Prospero's ruthless brother, **Antonio**, quite unmoved by the magic of the island or the chance of a new life, contemplates making money out of selling Caliban when he returns to Italy.

8. Before breaking his staff and drowning his magic books, **Prospero** boasts of the power he has wielded over the elements and spirits of the island.

9. This song celebrates the imminent freedom that Prospero has promised **Ariel**. When everyone else sets sail for Italy, Ariel will be free to enjoy his island world.

10. Whereas the shipwrecked courtiers see the island as a 'new world' – offering a potential way of life uncorrupted by civilisation – **Miranda**, having grown up on the island, sees a new world in the courtiers – dressed in all their finery. Alonso's court, however, represents the old world, the world which treated her father, Prospero so abominably. Prospero wryly comments 'Tis new to thee'.

A Brief Biography
of William Shakespeare

Although Shakespeare gave his name to the greatest period of English drama, his was an age when the art of the dramatist was not highly valued. Shakespeare did nothing to ensure that his plays were published and none of his contemporaries preserved biographical details. Official records reveal the following facts:

Shakespeare was baptised in Stratford-upon-Avon on 26th April 1564. His father, John Shakespeare, was a prominent citizen of Stratford and his mother, Mary Arden, was the daughter of a local land-owner. At the age of eighteen he married the twenty-six year old Anne Hathaway, who came from a neighbouring village. Six months later, a daughter, Susanna, was born. Twins, Hamnet and Judith, followed in 1585. Although Hamnet died at the age of eight, both daughters married and settled in Stratford. But the direct line of Shakespeare's descendents ended a generation later. Although Shakespeare spent most of his working life as an actor and dramatist in London, records show that he maintained regular contact with Stratford. He bought the second largest house in the town in 1597, retired there a decade or so later and died and was buried there in 1616. (Since Shakespeare's death was on 23rd April it has been traditional to celebrate both his birth and his death on that date.)

Contemporary references show that Shakespeare achieved early recognition as a poet and playwright, but it was not until 1623, seven years after his death, that two of his fellow actors, John Heminge and Henry Condell, collected his plays together and had them published in a single edition. Without the publication of this, The First Folio, some eighteen plays (including *Macbeth*, *Antony and Cleopatra* and *The Tempest*) would have been lost to posterity.

Since the publication of the First Folio there has been an abundance of speculation about Shakespeare. Much influenced by Alexander Pope – who produced his own edition of Shakespeare's plays in 1725 – the Augustans thought of him as a slightly crude, untutored genius. The Romantics, guided by Coleridge and Keats and by German scholarship, revered him for the power of his imagination, which they thought transcended his own and other ages. Towards the end of the nineteenth century it became fashionable to believe that his works contained sentiments too noble to have come from an ignorant burgher of Stratford (however powerful his imagination) and attempts were made to prove that the plays and poems had been written by Sir Francis Bacon. A host of other claimants have included the Earl of Oxford, Christopher Marlowe and Queen Elizabeth herself. But twentieth century scholarship has established a much sounder understanding of Elizabethan and Jacobean background, leaving William Shakespeare as the only credible author of his own works.

As the son of well-to-do parents, he would almost certainly have been educated at Stratford's Grammar School, where he would have received a solid grounding in Latin and the principles of rhetoric. Wide reading (of historical chronicles, translated classics, European romantic literature – as well as contemporary plays and poems) supplied him with a rich source of plots and characters. As a senior member of a leading London theatre company that catered for court performances as well as for the general London public, Shakespeare had freedom to develop his brilliant and varied stage-craft.

Recent research has focused on Shakespeare's links with the 'old' (Catholic) religion which had been driven underground during the reigns of Queen Elizabeth and James I. Although this has provided some fascinating insights into many aspects of the plays and poems, what finally impresses readers and theatre-goers is Shakespeare's ability to avoid narrow categorising and to stand as an artist of universal appeal.

Index of Plays and Poems